Bible Answers
for
Preschoolers

BARBOUR
PUBLISHING

ISBN 978-1-59789-942-0

Special thanks to Bonnie Jensen for her contribution to this project.

Published by Barbour Publishing, Inc., P.O. Box 719, Uhrichsville, Ohio 44683, www.barbourbooks.com

Our mission is to publish and distribute inspirational products offering exceptional value and biblical encouragement to the masses.

Member of the
Evangelical Christian
Publishers Association

Printed in the United States of America.

Anger

I need God's help
when I'm mad.
*He always
makes me feel better.*

Now is the time to get rid
of anger.

COLOSSIANS 3:8 NLT

A gentle answer turns away anger,
but a sharp word causes anger.

PROVERBS 15:1

Hot tempers start fights; a calm,
cool spirit keeps the peace.

PROVERBS 15:18 MSG

If you are angry, do not let it
become sin. Get over your anger
before the day is finished.

EPHESIANS 4:26

Smart people know how
to hold their tongue.

PROVERBS 19:11 MSG

Do not be quick in spirit
to be angry. For anger is
in the heart of fools.

ECCLESIASTES 7:9

Don't hang out with angry
people; don't keep company with
hotheads. Bad temper is
contagious—don't get infected.

PROVERBS 22:24–25 MSG

He who is slow to get angry has
great understanding.

PROVERBS 14:29

Stop being angry. Turn away from fighting. Do not trouble yourself. It leads only to wrong-doing.

PSALM 37:8

GOD is all mercy and grace—not quick to anger, is rich in love.

PSALM 145:8 MSG

Everyone should listen much and speak little. He should be slow to become angry.

JAMES 1:19

Work at getting along with each other and with God.

HEBREWS 12:14 MSG

Don't insist on getting even;
that's not for you to do.
"I'll do the judging," says God.
"I'll take care of it."

ROMANS 12:19 MSG

Do all things without arguing and
talking about how you wish
you did not have to do them. . . .
You are to shine as lights among
the sinful people of this world.

PHILIPPIANS 2:14–15

Wise men turn away anger.

PROVERBS 29:8

He who is slow to anger is better
than the powerful.

PROVERBS 16:32

A man who hurts people tempts
his neighbor to do the same,
and leads him in a way
that is not good.

PROVERBS 16:29

A dry piece of food with peace
and quiet is better than a house
full of food with fighting.

PROVERBS 17:1

Don't hit back.

ROMANS 12:19 MSG

Dear God,
When I get mad,
please help me to be nice.
Amen.

Courage

With God's help, I can do anything!

I can do all things because
Christ gives me the strength.

PHILIPPIANS 4:13

By not giving up, God's Word
gives us strength and hope.

ROMANS 15:4

"Peace I leave with you. My peace
I give to you. I do not give peace to
you as the world gives. Do not let
your hearts be troubled or afraid."

JOHN 14:27

You are my wonderful God
who gives me courage.

PSALM 3:3 ICB

Let us keep looking to Jesus. Our
faith comes from Him and He is
the One Who makes it perfect.

HEBREWS 12:2

"Come to Me, all of you who
work and have heavy loads.
I will give you rest."

MATTHEW 11:28

May [God] give your hearts
comfort and strength to say
and do every good thing.

2 THESSALONIANS 2:17

God has power over all
things forever.

1 PETER 5:11

I am happy to be weak and have
troubles so I can have Christ's
power in me. I receive joy when
I am weak. I receive joy when
people talk against me and make
it hard for me and try to hurt me
and make trouble for me. I receive
joy when all these things come to
me because of Christ. For when
I am weak, then I am strong.

2 CORINTHIANS 12:9–10

God. . .gives you strength.

ROMANS 15:5

We will receive [God's]
loving-kindness and have
His loving-favor to help
us whenever we need it.

HEBREWS 4:16

If we are sure [God] hears us
when we ask, we can be sure
He will give us what we ask for.

1 JOHN 5:15

"In the world you will have much
trouble. But take hope!
I have power over the world!"

JOHN 16:33

There is only one God.
He is the Father.
All things are from Him.
He made us for Himself.
There is one Lord.
He is Jesus Christ.
He made all things.
He keeps us alive.

1 CORINTHIANS 8:6

Dear God,
Thank You for helping me
be brave when I have to do
things that aren't easy.
Amen.

Faith

I believe in my heart
that God will do what
He says. That's faith!

You are all children of God
through faith in Christ Jesus.

GALATIANS 3:26 NLT

You must have faith as you
ask [God]. You must not doubt.
Anyone who doubts is like
a wave which is pushed
around by the sea.

JAMES 1:6

You have never seen [God] but you
love Him. You cannot see Him
now but you are putting your trust
in Him. And you have joy so great
that words cannot tell about it.

1 PETER 1:8

Now faith is being sure we will get what we hope for. It is being sure of what we cannot see.

HEBREWS 11:1

"Anything is possible if a person believes."

MARK 9:23 NLT

If we have no faith, [God] will still be faithful for He cannot go against what He is.

2 TIMOTHY 2:13

If you say with your mouth that Jesus is Lord, and believe in your heart that God raised Him from the dead, you will be saved from the punishment of sin.

ROMANS 10:9

Jesus said to him, "Thomas, because you have seen Me, you believe. Those are happy who have never seen Me and yet believe!"

JOHN 20:29

I will give thanks to the Lord with all my heart. I will tell of all the great things You have done.

PSALM 9:1

Let us come near to God
with a true heart full of faith.
Our hearts must be made clean
from guilty feelings and our
bodies washed with pure water.

HEBREWS 10:22

Get your strength from [Jesus].

COLOSSIANS 2:7

God makes all things work
together for the good of those
who love Him.

ROMANS 8:28

We can trust God that He
will do what He promised.

HEBREWS 10:23

Love the Lord,
all you who belong to Him!
The Lord keeps the faithful safe.

PSALM 31:23

[God] keeps His promise
and shows His lovingkindness
to those who love Him.

DEUTERONOMY 7:9

Be happy in the Lord. And He will
give you the desires of your heart.

PSALM 37:4

"I have loved you just as My Father
has loved Me. Stay in My love."

JOHN 15:9

And you must love the Lord
your God with all your heart
and with all your soul and
with all your strength.

DEUTERONOMY 6:5

You have turned my crying
into dancing. You have...
dressed me with joy.

PSALM 30:11

Dear God,
I have faith in
Your promises.
I know if You say it,
You'll do it!
Amen.

Fear

I don't ever need
to be afraid, because
God promises to protect
me and love me—always!

When I am afraid,
I will trust in [God].

PSALM 56:3

I will not be afraid because
the Lord is with me.

PSALM 118:6 ICB

Who can keep us away from the
love of Christ? Can trouble or
problems? ... [Nothing can]
keep us away from the love of
God which is ours through
Christ Jesus our Lord.

ROMANS 8:35, 39

"Do not be afraid! Be strong,
and see how the Lord
will save you today."

EXODUS 14:13

I will not be afraid of anything,
because [God is] with me.

PSALM 23:4

"See, God saves me. I will trust
and not be afraid. For the Lord
God is my strength and song."

ISAIAH 12:2

Do not be afraid.... Have joy
and be glad, for the Lord
has done great things.

JOEL 2:21

Do not fear, for I am with you.
Do not be afraid,
for I am your God.

ISAIAH 41:10

Those who do right do
not have to be afraid.

ROMANS 13:3

You will not be afraid when you
lie down. When you lie down,
your sleep will be sweet.

PROVERBS 3:24

"Do not be afraid. I am the
First and the Last."

REVELATION 1:17

"Be strong and have strength of heart! Do not be afraid or lose faith. For the Lord your God is with you anywhere you go."

JOSHUA 1:9

Do not be afraid. You are more important than many small birds.

MATTHEW 10:31

"I am with you to take you out of trouble," says the Lord.

JEREMIAH 1:8

"Do not be afraid, just believe."

MARK 5:36

Do not be afraid of
those who hate you.
PHILIPPIANS 1:28

"The Lord is my Helper.
I am not afraid of anything
man can do to me."
HEBREWS 13:6

God knows how many hairs
you have on your head.
Do not be afraid.
LUKE 12:7

[God said,] "Do not be afraid. . . .
You are Mine!"
ISAIAH 43:1

Dear God,
Thank You for
protecting me.
Because You are
always with me,
I don't ever have to be
afraid of anything!
Amen.

Forgiveness

When someone hurts my feelings and I forgive them, God is proud of me. I always want to make God happy.

"The forgiveness you give to others will be given to you."

MATTHEW 7:2 ICB

You must be kind to each other.
Think of the other person.
Forgive other people just
as God forgave you.

EPHESIANS 4:32

Forgive anyone who offends you.
Remember, the Lord forgave you,
so you must forgive others.

COLOSSIANS 3:13 NLT

"Do not fight with the man
who wants to fight."

MATTHEW 5:39

When someone does
something bad to you,
do not do the same thing to him.
When someone talks about you,
do not talk about him.
Instead, pray that good will
come to him. You were called
to do this so you might receive
good things from God.

1 PETER 3:9

"If one sinner is sorry for his sins
and turns from them,
the angels are very happy."

LUKE 15:10

"If you forgive people their sins, your Father in heaven will forgive your sins also."

MATTHEW 6:14

Peter came to Jesus and said, "Lord, how many times may my brother sin against me and I forgive him, up to seven times?" Jesus said to him, "I tell you, not seven times but seventy times seven!"

MATTHEW 18:21–22

"Forgive other people and other people will forgive you."

LUKE 6:37

For You are good and ready to
forgive, O Lord. You are
rich in loving-kindness
to all who call to You.

PSALM 86:5

The Lord does not want any
person to be punished forever.
He wants all people to
be sorry for their sins
and turn from them.

2 PETER 3:9

It will not go well for the man
who hides his sins, but he who
tells his sins and turns from them
will be given loving-pity.

PROVERBS 28:13

But you must be sorry for your
sins and turn from them.
You must turn to God and
have your sins taken away.
Then many times your soul
will receive new strength
from the Lord.

ACTS 3:19

You must be sorry for this sin
of yours and turn from it. Pray
to the Lord that He will forgive.

ACTS 8:22

Anyone who believes in God's
Son has eternal life.

JOHN 3:36 NLT

Anyone who belongs to Christ
has become a new person. The old
life is gone; a new life has begun!

2 CORINTHIANS 5:17 NLT

He washed away our sins, giving
us a new birth and new life
through the Holy Spirit.

TITUS 3:5 NLT

Become friends with God; he's
already a friend with you. How?
you ask. In Christ. God put the
wrong on him who never did
anything wrong, so we could
be put right with God.

2 CORINTHIANS 5:20–21 MSG

[God] wants all people to be saved
from the punishment of sin.
He wants them to come
to know the truth.

1 TIMOTHY 2:4

Dear God,
When someone hurts
my feelings, I need
Your help to forgive them.
And when I make a
mistake, thank You
for forgiving me!
Amen.

Friendship

God wants me to
be a good friend.
His Word shows
me how.

A friend loves at all times.

PROVERBS 17:17

"Do for other people what you
would like to have them
do for you."

LUKE 6:31

Think of other people as more
important than yourself.

PHILIPPIANS 2:3

A man who has friends
must be a friend.

PROVERBS 18:24

Love never comes to an end.

1 CORINTHIANS 13:8

Let us love each other,
because love comes from God.

1 JOHN 4:7

Help each other in troubles
and problems.

GALATIANS 6:2

"You are to love each other.
You must love each other
as I have loved you."

JOHN 13:34

Do not leave your
own friend. . .alone.

PROVERBS 27:10

"Treat people the same way you
want them to treat you."
MATTHEW 7:12 NASB

"No one can have greater love than
to give his life for his friends."
JOHN 15:13

If one falls down, his friend
can help him up.
ECCLESIASTES 4:10 NIV

We should do good to everyone.
GALATIANS 6:10

Dear God,
Thank You for my friends.
Help me to always treat
them just the way
I want to be treated.
Amen.

Happiness

My heart is always happy when I put my trust in God.

"Those who hear the Word
of God and obey it are happy."
LUKE 11:28

Be happy in the Lord.
PSALM 37:4

If someone has the gift of
showing kindness to others,
he should be happy as he does it.
ROMANS 12:8

Happy is the man who
cares for the poor.
PSALM 41:1

A glad heart makes a happy face.
PROVERBS 15:13

I am made happy
by [God's] Word.

PSALM 119:162

"Those who are hungry and thirsty
to be right with God are happy."

MATTHEW 5:6

Love is happy with the truth.

1 CORINTHIANS 13:6

Happy is the person who
trusts the Lord.

PSALM 40:4 ICB

"My heart is happy in the Lord."

1 SAMUEL 2:1

"Those who make peace are happy, because they will be called the sons of God."

MATTHEW 5:9

O taste and see that the Lord is good. How happy is the man who trusts in Him!

PSALM 34:8

We are happy for the hope we have of sharing the shining-greatness of God.

ROMANS 4:2

For You will make those happy who do what is right, O Lord.

PSALM 5:12

And my spirit is happy in God.

LUKE 1:47

"Those who show loving-kindness are happy, because they will have loving-kindness shown to them."

MATTHEW 5:7

"We are more happy when we give than when we receive."

ACTS 20:35

My soul will be happy in the Lord. It will be full of joy because He saves.

PSALM 35:9

"Those who have a pure heart
are happy, because
they will see God."
MATTHEW 5:8

Be happy in the Lord your God.
JOEL 2:23

Happy is the nation whose God
is the Lord. Happy are the people
He has chosen for His own.
PSALM 33:12

Dear God,
I know I can trust You
with all my heart.
That makes me happy!
Amen.

Heaven

Someday I will live
forever with
God in heaven.

"There is more than enough room in my Father's home. If this were not so, would I have told you that I am going to prepare a place for you? When everything is ready, I will come and get you, so that you will always be with me where I am."

JOHN 14:2–3 NLT

God is keeping careful watch over us and the future. The Day is coming when you'll have it all— life healed and whole.

1 PETER 1:5 MSG

There is a crown which comes
from being right with God.
The Lord, the One Who will
judge, will give it to me on that
great day when He comes again.

2 TIMOTHY 4:8

"My sheep hear My voice and I
know them. They follow Me.
I give them life that lasts forever.
They will never be punished.
No one is able to take them
out of My hand."

JOHN 10:27–28

God's free gift is life that lasts
forever. It is given to us by
our Lord Jesus Christ.

ROMANS 6:23

Our body is like a house
we live in here on earth.
When it is destroyed,
we know that God has another
body for us in heaven.
The new one will not be
made by human hands
as a house is made.
This body will last forever.

2 CORINTHIANS 5:1

Our human bodies made from
dust must be changed into a
body that cannot be destroyed.
Our human bodies that can die
must be changed into bodies
that will never die.

1 CORINTHIANS 15:53

"God will take away all tears
from their eyes."

REVELATION 7:17

We are looking for what God has
promised, which are new heavens
and a new earth. Only what is
right and good will be there.

2 PETER 3:13

If a man does things to please
his sinful old self, his soul
will be lost. If a man does things
to please the Holy Spirit,
he will have life that lasts forever.

<small>GALATIANS 6:8</small>

Jesus said. . . , "I am the One Who
raises the dead and gives them life.
Anyone who puts his trust in Me
will live again, even if he dies.
Anyone who lives and has put
his trust in Me will never die.
Do you believe this?"

<small>JOHN 11:25–26</small>

He will give eternal life to
those who keep on doing good,
seeking after the glory and honor
and immortality that God offers.

ROMANS 2:7 NLT

The Holy Spirit raised Jesus from
the dead. If the same Holy Spirit
lives in you, He will give life
to your bodies in the same way.

ROMANS 8:11

There will be no night [in heaven].
There will be no need for a light
or for the sun because the
Lord God will be their light.

REVELATION 22:5

"Anyone who hears My Word
and puts his trust in Him Who
sent Me has life that lasts forever.
He will not be guilty.
He has already passed
from death into life."

John 5:24

Christ has gone to heaven and is on
the right side of God. Angels and
powers of heaven are obeying Him.

1 Peter 3:22

The world and all its desires
will pass away. But the man who
obeys God and does what
He wants done will live forever.

1 John 2:17

We will receive the great things
that we have been promised.
They are being kept safe in
heaven for us. They are pure
and will not pass away.
They will never be lost.

1 PETER 1:4

"Why do you stand looking up
into heaven? This same Jesus
Who was taken from you into
heaven will return in the same way
you saw Him go up into heaven."

ACTS 1:11

Dear God,
Thank You for making
a home for me in heaven!
Amen.

Honesty

God wants me to tell
the truth—always.
*He never wants
me to tell a lie.*

The LORD. . .
delights in honesty.

PROVERBS 11:1 NLT

We want to do the right thing.
We want God and men
to know we are honest.

2 CORINTHIANS 8:21

Stand firm then, with the belt of
truth buckled around your waist.

EPHESIANS 6:14 NIV

The Lord gives favor and honor.
He holds back nothing good
from those who walk in
the way that is right.

PSALM 84:11

The Lord. . .delights in men
who are truthful.

Proverbs 12:22 niv

A little earned in a right way
is better than much earned
in a wrong way.

Proverbs 16:8

Dear children, let us not love
with words or tongue but
with actions and in truth.

1 John 3:18 niv

Good things will be given to
those who are right with God.

Proverbs 13:21

The Lord is near to all who
call on Him, to all who
call on Him in truth.

PSALM 145:18

Love does not delight in evil
but rejoices with the truth.

1 CORINTHIANS 13:6 NIV

Speak the truth to each other.

ZECHARIAH 8:16 NIV

I have no greater joy than
to hear that my children
are walking in the truth.

3 JOHN 1:4 NIV

"Do not lie."

For You will make those happy
who do what is right, O Lord.

Do not do wrong to one another.

Dear God,
I will be honest
because I know it
makes You happy!
Amen.

Hope

My hope comes from God
and His promises to me.
He has only the best
things planned for me.

Hope means we are waiting for something we do not have.

ROMANS 8:24

I will put my hope in God!

PSALM 42:11 NLT

Dear friends, we are already God's children.

1 JOHN 3:2 NLT

We know that troubles help us learn not to give up. When we have learned not to give up, it shows we have stood the test. When we have stood the test, it gives us hope.

ROMANS 5:3–4

The hope of the righteous
will be gladness.

PROVERBS 10:28 NKJV

Because Jesus was raised from
the dead, we've been given a
brand-new life and have
everything to live for,
including a future in heaven.

1 PETER 1:3 MSG

Good will come to the man
who trusts in the Lord,
and whose hope is in the Lord.

JEREMIAH 17:7

We believe that Jesus died and
then came to life again. Because
we believe this, we know that
God will bring to life again
all those who belong to Jesus.

1 Thessalonians 4:14

You are my hiding place. . . .
I put my hope in Your Word.

Psalm 119:114

It's a good thing to quietly hope,
quietly hope for help from God.

Lamentations 3:26 msg

I have put my hope
in [God's] Word.

Psalm 119:81

This truth also gives hope of life that lasts forever. God promised this before the world began. He cannot lie.

TITUS 1:2

We are of God's house if we keep our trust in the Lord until the end. This is our hope.

HEBREWS 3:6

We who have turned to [God] can have great comfort knowing that He will do what He has promised. This hope is a safe anchor for our souls. It will never move.

HEBREWS 6:18–19

Our hope comes from God.
May He fill you with joy and
peace because of your trust in
Him. May your hope grow
stronger by the power
of the Holy Spirit.

ROMANS 15:13

I hope for Your saving power,
O Lord, and I follow Your Word.

PSALM 119:166

We speak without fear because
our trust is in Christ.

2 CORINTHIANS 3:12

I pray that you will know about
the hope given by God's call.
I pray that you will see how
great the things are that
He has promised to those
who belong to Him.

EPHESIANS 1:18

I hope very much that I will
have no reason to be ashamed.
I hope to honor Christ
with my body. . . .
I want to honor Him
without fear, now and always.

PHILIPPIANS 1:20

Why am I discouraged? Why is my heart so sad? I will put my hope in God! I will praise him again—my Savior and my God!

Psalm 42:11 NLT

We thank God for the hope that is being kept for you in heaven. You first heard about this hope through the Good News which is the Word of Truth.

Colossians 1:5

Now faith is being sure we will get what we hope for. It is being sure of what we cannot see.

Hebrews 11:1

Dear God,
My hope is in You
and Your promises.
Thank You for being
so good to me!
Amen.

Hurts

God will always be here
for me when I'm hurt.
He will make
my hurts better.

Because I suffer and am in need,
let the Lord think of me. You are
my help and the One Who sets
me free. O my God, do not wait.

PSALM 40:17

[The Lord said,] "In this world
you will have trouble. But take
heart! I have overcome the world."

JOHN 16:33 NIV

The little troubles we suffer now
for a short time are making us
ready for the great things God
is going to give us forever.

2 CORINTHIANS 4:17

[Jesus said,] "Come to Me...
and...I will give you rest."
MATTHEW 11:28

We know that God makes all
things work together for the good
of those who love Him and are
chosen to be a part of His plan.
ROMANS 8:28

Even if I walk into trouble,
[God] will keep my life safe.
PSALM 138:7

Give all your worries to [God]
because He cares for you.
1 PETER 5:7

I call to God; God will help me.

PSALM 55:17 MSG

"Those who have sorrow are happy,
because they will be comforted."

MATTHEW 5:4

Is anyone among you suffering?
He should pray.

JAMES 5:13

"You are sad now. I will see you
again and then your hearts will
be full of joy. No one can
take your joy from you."

JOHN 16:22

God is our safe place.
PSALM 46:1

[God] gives us comfort
in all our troubles.
2 CORINTHIANS 1:4

Give all your cares to the Lord
and He will give you strength.
PSALM 55:22

Our Lord Jesus Christ and
God our Father loves us.
Through His loving-favor
He gives us comfort and
hope that lasts forever.
2 THESSALONIANS 2:16

The Lord is good,
a safe place in times of trouble.
And He knows those
who come to Him to be safe.

Nahum 1:7

I am sure that our suffering
now cannot be compared to
the shining-greatness that
[God] is going to give us.

Romans 8:18

When he falls, he will not be
thrown down, because the
Lord holds his hand.

Psalm 37:24

Dear God,
Thank You for coming
to my rescue when I'm
hurt. You always know
just what I need when
I'm feeling down.
Amen.

Kindness

God wants me to be kind to others so they can see *His* love in me.

Don't ever stop being kind. . . .
Let kindness and truth
show in all you do.

PROVERBS 3:3 ICB

"Give to any person who asks
you for something. If a person
takes something from you,
do not ask for it back."

LUKE 6:30

Each of us should live
to please his neighbor.
This will help him grow in faith.

ROMANS 15:2

When someone does something bad to you, do not do the same thing to him. When someone talks about you, do not talk about him. Instead, pray that good will come to him. You were called to do this so you might receive good things from God.

1 Peter 3:9

God has chosen you. You are holy and loved by Him. Because of this, your new life should be full of loving-pity. You should be kind to others and have no pride. Be gentle and be willing to wait for others.

Colossians 3:12

"You must have loving-kindness just as your Father has loving-kindness."

LUKE 6:36

The Lord. . .said, "Do what is right and be kind and show loving-pity to one another. . . . Do not make sinful plans in your hearts against one another."

ZECHARIAH 7:9–10

"Love your enemies! Do good to them. . . . Then your reward from heaven will be very great, and you will truly be acting as children of [God]."

LUKE 6:35 NLT

Laugh with your happy friends
when they're happy; share tears
when they're down.

ROMANS 12:15 MSG

We should do good to everyone.
For sure, we should do good
to those who belong to Christ.

GALATIANS 6:10

Be kind to Christian brothers
and love them.

2 PETER 1:7

He who hates his neighbor sins,
but happy is he who shows
lovingfavor to the poor.

PROVERBS 14:21

"Give to any person who asks you for something. Do not say no to the man who wants to use something of yours."

MATTHEW 5:42

Anyone who shows no loving-kindness will have no loving-kindness shown to him when he is told he is guilty. But if you show loving-kindness, God will show loving-kindness to you when you are told you are guilty.

JAMES 2:13

Those who follow this way
will have God's peace and
loving-kindness. They are the
people of God.

GALATIANS 6:16

The loving-kindness of the Lord
is given to the people of all
times who honor Him.

LUKE 1:50

"Those who show loving-kindness
are happy, because they will have
loving-kindness shown to them."

MATTHEW 5:7

Dear God,
I want to be kind,
showing Your love
to others every day!
Amen.

Loneliness

When I feel alone,
I can talk to God.
He's always here for me.

"I am with you always."

MATTHEW 28:20

"I am with you.
No one will hurt you."

ACTS 18:10

You will look for the Lord your
God. And you will find Him
if you look for Him with
all your heart and soul.

DEUTERONOMY 4:29

When you pass through
the waters, I will be with you.

ISAIAH 43:2

"The Lord knows those
who are His."

2 TIMOTHY 2:19

The eyes of the Lord watch over
those who do right.

1 PETER 3:12 NLT

[The Lord said,] "See, I am
with you. I will care for you
everywhere you go."

GENESIS 28:15

I will not be afraid of anything,
because You are with me.

PSALM 23:4

God has said, "I will never
leave you or let you be alone."

HEBREWS 13:5

Then you will call, and the Lord
will answer. You will cry,
and He will say, "Here I am."

ISAIAH 58:9

"The Lord is with you when you
are with Him. If you look for Him,
He will let you find Him."

2 CHRONICLES 15:2

If you live in love, you live by the
help of God and God lives in you.

1 JOHN 4:16

"I will be a Father to you,
and you will be my
sons and daughters,
says the Lord Almighty."

2 CORINTHIANS 6:18 NIV

[God said,] I've called your name.
You're mine.

ISAIAH 43:4 MSG

[God] is not far from
each one of us.

ACTS 17:27

Dear God,
I never need to feel alone.
You are always here
to make me feel
safe and special.
You love me—
Your Word tells me so!
Amen.

Love

God's love for me
is so big,
I can't even measure it.

If God so loved us, we also
ought to love one another.

1 JOHN 4:11 NKJV

God has shown His love to us by
sending His only Son into the
world. God did this so we might
have life through Christ.

1 JOHN 4:9

"No eye has ever seen or no ear
has ever heard or no mind has ever
thought of the wonderful things
God has made ready for those
who love Him."

1 CORINTHIANS 2:9

For I know that nothing
can keep us from the
love of God.

ROMANS 8:38

Love each other as Christian
brothers. Show respect
for each other.

ROMANS 12:10

The love of God has come into our
hearts through the Holy Spirit
Who was given to us.

ROMANS 5:5

The Lord takes care of
all who love Him.

PSALM 145:20

God is love. If you live in love,
you live by the help of God
and God lives in you.

1 JOHN 4:16

You obey [God] when you do this
one thing, "Love your neighbor
as you love yourself."

GALATIANS 5:14

This is love! It is not that we
loved God but that He loved us.
For God sent His Son to pay for
our sins with His own blood.

1 JOHN 4:10

God has taught you to
love each other.

1 THESSALONIANS 4:9

God so loved the world that
He gave His only Son.

JOHN 3:16

God showed His love to us.
While we were still sinners,
Christ died for us.

ROMANS 5:8

Dear friends, if God loved us
that much, then we should
love each other.

1 JOHN 4:11

We have these three: faith
and hope and love, but the
greatest of these is love.

1 CORINTHIANS 13:13

"This is what I tell you to do: Love
each other just as I have loved you.
No one can have greater love than
to give his life for his friends."

JOHN 15:12–13

"You are to love each other.
You must love each other as
I have loved you. If you love each
other, all men will know you
are My followers."

JOHN 13:34–35

Love each other with a kind
heart and with a mind
that has no pride.

1 PETER 3:8

The Lord came to us from far
away, saying, "I have loved you
with a love that lasts forever.
So I have helped you come to
Me with loving-kindness."

JEREMIAH 31:3

"I have loved you just as
My Father has loved Me.
Stay in My love."

JOHN 15:9

" 'You must love the Lord
your God with all your heart
and with all your soul
and with all your mind.'
This is the first
and greatest of the Laws.
The second is like it,
'You must love your neighbor
as you love yourself.'"

MATTHEW 22:37–39

Dear God,
Please help me love others
as much as You love me!
Amen.

Obedience

Obedience is a very big word! It means to do what God's Word says. Doing what God says shows just how much I love Him.

We are taught to have nothing
to do with that which is against
God. We are to have nothing to
do with the desires of this world.
We are to be wise and to be
right with God. We are to live
God-like lives in this world.

TITUS 2:12

Those who obey what they
have been taught are happy.

PROVERBS 29:18 ICB

"Let your light shine in front of
men. Then they will see the good
things you do and will honor
your Father Who is in heaven."

MATTHEW 5:16

God is helping you obey Him.
God is doing what
He wants done in you.

PHILIPPIANS 2:13

For if a man belongs to Christ,
he is a new person. The old life
is gone. New life has begun.

2 CORINTHIANS 5:17

"The one who loves Me is the one
who has My teaching and obeys it."

JOHN 14:21

Remember this,
whatever good thing you do,
the Lord will pay you for it.

EPHESIANS 6:8

So give yourselves to God.
Stand against the devil and
he will run away from you.

JAMES 4:7

We will receive from Him
whatever we ask if we obey Him
and do what He wants.

1 JOHN 3:22

Children. . .obey your parents.
This is the right thing to do.

EPHESIANS 6:1

We take hold of every thought
and make it obey Christ.

2 CORINTHIANS 10:5

Do not. . .get tired of doing good.
If we do not give up,
we will get what is coming
to us at the right time.

GALATIANS 6:9

You are being made more like
Christ. He is the One
Who made you.

COLOSSIANS 3:10

The man who obeys God
and does what He wants
done will live forever.

1 JOHN 2:17

Have your roots planted deep
in Christ. Grow in Him.
Get your strength from Him.
Let Him make you strong in the
faith as you have been taught.

COLOSSIANS 2:7

Children, obey your parents
in everything. The Lord is
pleased when you do.

COLOSSIANS 3:20

Always do your work well for
the Lord. You know that
whatever you do for Him
will not be wasted.

1 CORINTHIANS 15:58

Dear God,
I want to obey
Your Word every day
in everything I do.
Amen.

Patience

I will be patient and
trust God—
always waiting with
a happy heart.

Patience and encouragement
come from God.

ROMANS 15:5 ICB

Rest in the Lord and
be willing to wait for Him.

PSALM 37:7

You must be willing to wait
without giving up. After you
have done what God wants you
to do, God will give you what
He promised you.

HEBREWS 10:36

Do not let yourselves get
tired of doing good.

GALATIANS 6:9

God's people need to keep
true to God's Word and
stay faithful to Jesus.

REVELATION 14:12

Learn well how to wait so you
will be strong and complete
and in need of nothing.

JAMES 1:4

We are glad for our troubles also.
We know that troubles help us
learn not to give up. When we have
learned not to give up, it shows we
have stood the test. When we have
stood the test, it gives us hope.

ROMANS 5:3–4

The God Who helps you not
to give up and gives you strength
will help you think so you
can please each other
as Christ Jesus did.

ROMANS 15:5

May the Lord lead your hearts
into the love of God. May He
help you as you wait for Christ.

2 THESSALONIANS 3:5

Be willing to wait for the Lord
to come again. . . . Be strong in
your hearts because the Lord
is coming again soon.

JAMES 5:7–8

Do not be lazy. Be like those who
have faith and have not given up.
They will receive what God
has promised them.

HEBREWS 6:12

Do not be quick in spirit to
be angry. For anger is in
the heart of fools.

ECCLESIASTES 7:9

For we belong to Christ if we keep
on trusting Him to the end just
as we trusted Him at first.

HEBREWS 3:14

Let us hold on to the hope we say we have and not be changed. We can trust God that He will do what He promised.

HEBREWS 10:23

Let us keep looking to Jesus. Our faith comes from Him and He is the One Who makes it perfect. He did not give up when He had to suffer shame and die on a cross. He knew of the joy that would be His later. Now He is sitting at the right side of God.

HEBREWS 12:2

But the fruit that comes from
having the Holy Spirit in our lives
is: love, joy, peace, not giving up,
being kind, being good, having
faith, being gentle, and being
the boss over our own desires.

GALATIANS 5:22–23

God has chosen you. You are holy
and loved by Him. Because of this,
your new life should be full of
loving-pity. You should be kind to
others and have no pride.
Be gentle and be willing
to wait for others.

COLOSSIANS 3:12

Use the Word of God to help
them do right. You must be
willing to wait for people to
understand what you teach
as you teach them.

2 TIMOTHY 4:2

A man with a bad temper
starts fights, but he who is slow
to anger quiets fighting.

PROVERBS 15:18

It is good that one should be
quiet and wait for the saving
power of the Lord.

LAMENTATIONS 3:26

Dear God,
It's hard to be patient.
Please help me wait
with a smile on my face.
Amen.

Prayer

Whenever I pray,
God is always listening.
He never goes to sleep!

Learn to pray about everything.
Give thanks to God as you ask
Him for what you need.

PHILIPPIANS 4:6

Whatever you ask for when
you pray, have faith that you will
receive it. Then you will get it.

MARK 11:24

God's there, listening for all who
pray, for all who pray and mean it.

PSALM 145:18 MSG

[God said,] "When you call
on me, when you come and
pray to me, I'll listen."

JEREMIAH 29:12 MSG

"If you get your life from Me
and My Words live in you,
ask whatever you want.
It will be done for you."

John 15:7

"When you pray, go into a room
by yourself. After you have shut
the door, pray to your Father
Who is in secret. Then your
Father Who sees in secret
will reward you."

Matthew 6:6

"Ask, and what you are asking
for will be given to you."

Matthew 7:7

We are sure that if we ask
anything that [God] wants us to
have, He will hear us. If we are
sure He hears us when we ask,
we can be sure He will give
us what we ask for.

1 JOHN 5:14–15

Pray for the things that are needed.
You must watch and keep on
praying. Remember to pray
for all Christians.

EPHESIANS 6:18

The Lord listens when
I pray to Him.

PSALM 4:3 ICB

The prayer from the heart
of a man right with God
has much power.

JAMES 5:16

We will receive from Him
whatever we ask if we obey
Him and do what He wants.

1 JOHN 3:22

Let us give thanks all the time to
God through Jesus Christ.
Our gift to Him is to give thanks.

HEBREWS 13:15

"Your Father knows what you
need before you ask Him."

MATTHEW 6:8

"Whatever you ask in My name, I will do it so the shining-greatness of the Father may be seen in the Son. Yes, if you ask anything in My name, I will do it."

JOHN 14:13-14

"All things you ask for in prayer, you will receive if you have faith."

MATTHEW 21:22

I ask you to pray much for all men and to give thanks for them.

1 TIMOTHY 2:1

Dear God,
I'm so glad that I can
talk to You. You always
hear my prayers.
Thank You for
loving me so much.
Amen.

Sharing

God has given me
so much. I can share
with others!

And I thingk
God is nisa

[You] should give much to those in need and be ready to share.

1 Timothy 6:18

"When you have a supper, ask poor people. Ask those who cannot walk and those who are blind. You will be happy if you do this. They cannot pay you back. You will get your reward when the people who are right with God are raised from the dead."

Luke 14:13–14

"If you have two coats, give one to him who has none. If you have food, you must share some."

Luke 3:11

God can give you all you need.
He will give you more than
enough. You will have everything
you need for yourselves. And you
will have enough left over to give
when there is a need.

2 Corinthians 9:8

God loves a man who gives
because he wants to give.

2 Corinthians 9:7

"When you give, do not let your
left hand know what your right
hand gives. Your giving should be
in secret. Then your Father Who
sees in secret will reward you."

Matthew 6:3–4

If your brother becomes poor
and is not able to pay you what
he owes, then you should help
him as you would help
a stranger or visitor.

LEVITICUS 25:35

Be free in giving
to your brother, to those in need,
and to the poor in your land.

DEUTERONOMY 15:11

Happy is the man
who cares for the poor.
The Lord will save him
in times of trouble.

PSALM 41:1

Every man should give as
he is able, as the Lord
your God has given to you.

DEUTERONOMY 16:17

"Give, and it will be given to you.
You will have more than
enough. . . . The way you give
to others is the way you
will receive in return."

LUKE 6:38

He who shows kindness to a poor
man gives to the Lord and He will
pay him in return for his good act.

PROVERBS 19:17

We must remember what
the Lord Jesus said,
"We are more happy when we
give than when we receive."

ACTS 20:35

God will give you enough so
you can always give to others.
Then many will give thanks to
God for sending gifts through us.

2 CORINTHIANS 9:11

Dear God,
Help me to remember
that everything I have
is a gift from You.
Help me share these
gifts with others.
Amen.

I will start my prayers
with a great big
"Thank You" to God,
because *He* is
so good to me.

I will give thanks to the Lord
with all my heart. I will tell of all
the great things You have done.

PSALM 9:1

Always give thanks for all things
to God the Father in the name
of our Lord Jesus Christ.

EPHESIANS 5:20

I will speak with the voice
of thanks, and tell of all
Your great works.

PSALM 26:7

Give thanks to the LORD,
for He is good!

PSALM 136:1 NKJV

"O give thanks to the Lord.
Call upon His name. Let the
people know what He has done."

1 Chronicles 16:8

In everything give thanks.
This is what God wants you
to do because of Christ Jesus.

1 Thessalonians 5:18

Do not be guilty of telling bad
stories and of foolish talk.
These things are not for you to do.
Instead, you are to give thanks
for what God has done for you.

Ephesians 5:4

Thank God for His great Gift.

2 CORINTHIANS 9:15

Give thanks to God in the
meetings of worship.

PSALM 68:26

I will give thanks to the Lord
because He is right and good.
I will sing praise to the name
of the Lord Most High.

PSALM 7:17

I thank Christ Jesus our Lord
for the power and strength He
has given me. He trusted me
and gave me His work to do.

1 TIMOTHY 1:12

Give thanks to God as you ask
Him for what you need.

PHILIPPIANS 4:6

Everything God made is good.
We should not put anything
aside if we can take it and
thank God for it.

1 TIMOTHY 4:4

We give thanks to You, O God.
We give thanks that Your name
is near. Men tell about the
great things You have done.

PSALM 75:1

Jesus looked up and said, "Father,
I thank You for hearing Me."

JOHN 11:41

I always thank God when
I speak of you in my prayers.

PHILEMON 1:4

Let us honor and thank the God
and Father of our Lord Jesus
Christ. He has already given
us a taste of what heaven is like.

EPHESIANS 1:3

Your life should be full
of thanks to [God].

COLOSSIANS 2:7

Let us thank the God and
Father of our Lord Jesus Christ.
It was through His loving-
kindness that we were born
again to a new life and have
a hope that never dies.
This hope is ours because
Jesus was raised from the dead.

1 PETER 1:3

Let the peace of Christ have
power over your hearts.
You were chosen as a part of
His body. Always be thankful.

COLOSSIANS 3:15

Dear God,
Thank You for all the
good things You give me.
I love You, God!
Amen.

Worry

Even when I can't be
in charge of things
that happen, God doesn't
want me to worry—
He wants me to let Him
take care of everything.

"I tell you this:
Do not worry about your life.
Do not worry about what
you are going to eat and drink.
Do not worry about what you
are going to wear. Is not life
more important than food?
Is not the body more
important than clothes?"

MATTHEW 6:25

Do not worry. Learn to pray
about everything. Give thanks
to God as you ask Him
for what you need.

PHILIPPIANS 4:6

"Which of you can make himself a little taller by worrying? Why should you worry about clothes? Think how the flowers grow. They do not work or make cloth. But I tell you that Solomon in all his greatness was not dressed as well as one of these flowers."

MATTHEW 6:27–29

I know that nothing can keep us from the love of God.

ROMANS 8:38

God will give you everything you need because of His great riches in Christ Jesus.

PHILIPPIANS 4:19

"Do not worry about tomorrow.
Tomorrow will have its own
worries. The troubles we have
in a day are enough for one day."
MATTHEW 6:34

You have turned my crying into
dancing. . . . So my soul may sing
praise to You, and not be quiet.
O Lord my God, I will
give thanks to You forever.
PSALM 30:11–12

Thanks be to the Lord,
Who carries our heavy loads day
by day. He is the God
Who saves us.
PSALM 68:19

The peace of God is much greater than the human mind can understand. This peace will keep your hearts and minds through Christ Jesus.

<small>PHILIPPIANS 4:7</small>

It is good to give thanks to the Lord, and sing praises to Your name, O Most High. It is good to tell of Your loving-kindness in the morning, and of how faithful You are at night.

<small>PSALM 92:1–2</small>

God did not keep His own Son
for Himself but gave Him for
us all. Then with His Son,
will He not give us all things?

ROMANS 8:32

There is no wisdom and no
understanding and no words that
can stand against the Lord.

PROVERBS 21:30

God is faithful.
He will not allow you to be
tempted more than you can take.
But when you are tempted,
He will make a way for you to
keep from falling into sin.

1 CORINTHIANS 10:13

"Peace I leave with you.
My peace I give to you.
I do not give peace to you as the
world gives. Do not let your hearts
be troubled or afraid."

JOHN 14:27

If you follow Christ. . .
God will be happy with you.
Men will think well of you also.
Work for the things that make
peace and help each other
become stronger Christians.

ROMANS 14:18–19

Dear God,
Thank You for taking
my worries away.
Amen.